The Locked Door

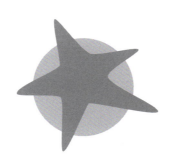

Maverick

Chapter Readers

'The Locked Door'
An original concept by Jill Atkins
© Jill Atkins 2022

Illustrated by Miriam Serafin

Published by MAVERICK ARTS PUBLISHING LTD
Studio 11, City Business Centre, 6 Brighton Road,
Horsham, West Sussex, RH13 5BB
© Maverick Arts Publishing Limited May 2022
+44 (0)1403 256941

A CIP catalogue record for this book is available at the British Library.

ISBN 978-1-84886-886-1

www.maverickbooks.co.uk

Grey

This book is rated as: Grey Band (Guided Reading)

The Locked Door

Written by
Jill Atkins

Illustrated by
Miriam Serafin

Chapter 1

Izzy stood at the rickety, old gate and looked up at the house. It was odd how narrow it was, with the wide expanse of rough ground to one side. The tall, dark windows seemed to be watching her. She shivered, then began to walk along the uneven stone path towards the oak front door.

"Wait for me!" shouted Tom, racing to catch her up.

Izzy stopped and turned.

"Do you remember coming here before?" she asked.

"Yes, just about," said Tom. "A long time ago."

Izzy nodded then shivered again. There was something about the house that she couldn't quite explain.

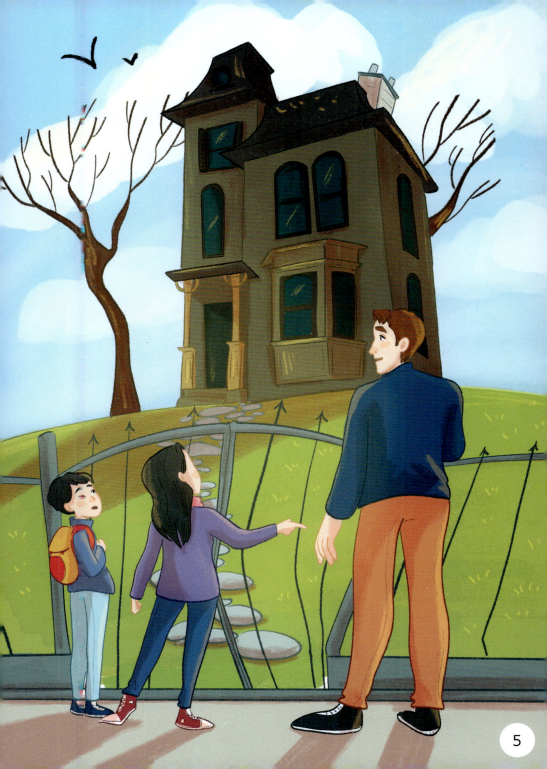

"We were quite small," she said. "But I remember the stairs—very dark and narrow."

"Yes, and cobwebs!" laughed Tom.

Dad caught them up and they walked to the door. Dad lifted the large lion's head knocker. **Thud! Thud!** The sound echoed inside the house.

"Do you think Great Aunt Winifred is at home?" Izzy asked, feeling rather jittery about going inside now they were here.

"I hope so," Dad replied. "She said she would have tea ready when we arrived."

After a moment, Izzy heard shuffling footsteps and the door creaked open. She took a big breath and tried to relax.

"Come in, come in," came a high-pitched voice from the gloomy hallway. "The kettle is boiling and I've got cakes from the baker and..."

"Thank you, Aunt," said Dad as he stepped inside.

Izzy and Tom followed.

The little, grey-haired woman who came out of the shadows was just as Izzy remembered, except she seemed smaller than before.

Immediately, the slightly damp, musty smell of the house brought back vivid memories of the last time they had come. They had been allowed to explore the house; downstairs were the front room, kitchen, and a tiny old-fashioned bathroom and toilet out in the backyard. Then they had climbed the rickety stairs to the two bedrooms: one of which was Great Aunt Winifred's, and the other, smaller one she called the spare room.

"Do you remember?" whispered Tom.

Izzy smiled and nodded.

"It's lovely to see you," said Great Aunt Winifred. "You've both grown so much. Izzy, quite the young lady with that lovely long, dark hair! Ten, are you?"

Izzy nodded shyly.

"Sit down. Let's have some tea."

They were herded into the front room and sat at a

round table that was covered in a dark red velvet cloth. Izzy looked at Tom. He looked nervous but, as soon as they had eaten a delicious chocolate cake and drunk a cup of tea, he was grinning and Izzy felt herself relax.

"I like to have visitors," said Great Aunt Winifred with cake crumbs spilling out all over her chin. "I'm all alone here, you know... well, except for the ghost."

"Ghost?" Izzy and Tom exclaimed together.

"Oh yes. The house is haunted. Has been ever since I've lived here and that's over fifty years."

Izzy almost choked on her tea. She knew there was something mysterious about the place.

"Oh, I almost forgot," said Great Aunt Winifred before Izzy could ask anything. "I wanted to show you an interesting book. It's upstairs in the spare room. Would you mind fetching it for me?"

Izzy and Tom stayed close together as they climbed the stairs.

"A ghost!" whispered Tom. "I wonder if we'll meet it."

Izzy glanced around her.

"I wonder where it is now," she whispered.

"Do you think it's a friendly ghost?" asked Tom.

"Well, it hasn't done Great Aunt Winifred any harm."

But Izzy jumped at every creak of the stairs and stood outside the spare room door for a while before she dared open it. The room was empty except for some old boxes, a rolled-up carpet, and a little table in front of the fireplace.

"No ghost here!" laughed Tom.

"That's a relief!" said Izzy. "Let's find that book and take it downstairs."

Suddenly, she froze. "Did you hear that?"

"What?"

There it was again, slightly louder this time. She held up her finger.

"Listen."

Tom gasped. "I can hear it now... a low, moaning sound."

Izzy nodded.

"Where's it coming from?" asked Tom.

Izzy pointed.

"From behind that door," she whispered. Then her hands flew to her mouth. "That door!" she repeated.

"What about it?"

"It wasn't here before. Don't you remember? We played hide and seek last time we came and I was disappointed there weren't any hiding places in this room."

Chapter 2

They both stared at the door.

"How can a door suddenly appear?" whispered Tom.

Izzy shrugged her shoulders. "How should I know?" she said. "There aren't any more rooms in Great Aunt Winifred's narrow house, so why is it here?"

"Perhaps it's a cupboard," said Tom.

Izzy shrugged. "We might as well open it and see."

Tom frowned.

"What if the ghost is in there?" he said.

"We'll be alright," Izzy said. She stepped forward and nervously turned the door handle. But the door wouldn't budge.

"It's locked. I wonder if there's a key."

They searched under the table, in the boxes, and even unrolled the carpet, but found no key.

"Let's check the floorboards," said Izzy, but there were no loose boards where a key could be hidden. "It must be somewhere."

At last, she noticed one of the fireplace tiles was sticking out about a centimetre. She hurried over to it.

"Got it!" She pulled out a little brass key from behind the tile. With shaking hands, she tried it in the lock. It fitted perfectly and, with a loud click, it turned.

Tom stood behind Izzy while she slowly pushed the door.

She stared in utter amazement.

"How on earth...?"

"Wow!" whispered Tom.

The door had opened into a large, elegant sitting room. Izzy gazed at the patterned carpets, red armchairs, red velvet curtains hanging at long windows, and the large paintings hanging on the walls.

At that moment, she heard the moaning sound again. It was louder now and there was a strange, jangling sound too.

"Come on," said Izzy. "Let's go and investigate."

Tom gripped her hand.

"I don't like it. Are you sure we'll be alright?"

"There's only one way to find out!" said Izzy, and she tiptoed into the room.

Glancing from side to side, they slowly crossed the room. Izzy's whole body was tense, ready to dash back into Great Aunt Winifred's house, but there was no sign of a ghost anywhere. The moaning and jangling sounds were gradually growing louder, but she couldn't let Tom know how scared she was. She had to look after him He was younger than her, but his presence right behind her gave her courage.

At the end of the room, they came to another door.

"What now?" whispered Tom.

"Let's carry on," Izzy whispered back. "That moaning

sounds almost like someone is trying to say something."

"Yeah. Creepy!"

The door opened onto another large room.

"The dining room!" whispered Tom. "Look! The table is laid for dinner."

Izzy stared. Tom was right. The long, shiny wood table was covered with silver cutlery, white crockery and crystal glasses. There were twelve chairs around it.

"It looks as if there's going to be a dinner party," she whispered.

"I hope the people don't arrive now!" said Tom, looking around.

But no one came, and they soon found themselves on a wide landing.

"Look, there are six more doors," said Izzy.

"They might be bedrooms," said Tom.

"Yes, but let's follow the sound. It's coming from down there."

She pointed to the grand, curved staircase that swept

down into a wide hallway.

As soon as they reached the ground floor, Izzy felt a cold draught. It was as if an icy finger was sliding up her spine. She was sure it came from the door to her right and that was definitely where the sounds were coming from too.

Clenching her teeth together to stop them chattering, she took Tom's hand and gave him a little tug.

"Come on."

"But Dad will wonder where we've got to. Shall we go back?"

"No. We've come this far. We can't give up now."

"Aren't you scared?" Tom asked.

Izzy shrugged. "I'm more curious than scared." She wouldn't admit to him that her legs were shaking and her mouth was dry. She didn't want to turn back.

They hurried through the door into a wide kitchen with a large, wooden table in the middle, copper pots and pans on high shelves and an enormous black oven. Dark stone steps led down from the kitchen. Down they crept, holding on to damp walls, until they reached yet another door. Izzy reached out and touched the rough wood.

"This must be the cellar," she whispered, but her voice shook. "I don't know if I dare go in."

But at that moment, the door slowly creaked open by itself.

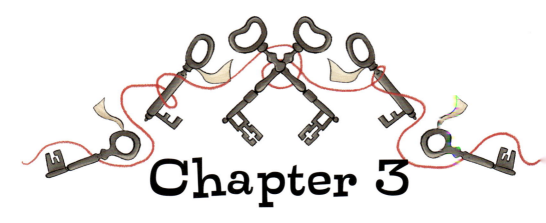

Chapter 3

Tom turned to run away, but Izzy grabbed his arm.

"Don't go, please," she pleaded. "Okay, I'll admit it. I'm terrified, just like you, but I don't want to give up yet. I'm still curious."

They peered into a room that was as black as coal.

"Can't see a thing," whispered Tom.

Izzy put her hand in her pocket and pulled out her phone.

"It's got a torch," she said.

As soon as she turned on the torch, its beam lit up a few shapes which made enormous shadows on the walls.

She directed the torch beam slowly around the room and stopped on each object.

"Barrels!" she gasped. "Do you think they're full of wine?"

"Probably!" said Tom as the torch shone on some rusty machinery.

Then the light swung onto a big, wooden chest.

"I wonder what's in there," said Izzy. "Let's have a look."

As they approached the chest, there was a loud moan which stopped them in their tracks. Izzy was torn. She was scared out of her wits and desperately wanted to go back. How did she know this ghost was as harmless as Great Aunt Winifred had said?

But her curiosity was so strong. She really wanted to find out more.

The moaning stopped. Everywhere was eerily silent.

"Let's just peep in the chest," she whispered close to Tom's ear. "Then we can go."

"Alright," said Tom.

Together, they lifted the heavy lid.

"Clothes!" gasped Izzy.

"Boring!" said Tom.

"No, look. They're very old fashioned." She pulled a blue, silk dress from the chest and held it up against her. "And very grand," she added.

Tom found a tall, cylinder-shaped box and lifted the lid.

"Look at this!" he gasped, pulling out a tall top hat and putting it on. It was so big it covered most of his face.

Izzy laughed.

They pulled out more grand clothes, some black shoes with a row of buttons, and a lady's hat with feathers.

"I think they're Victorian," said Izzy. "So they're well over a hundred years old. I wonder who they belonged to."

"Maybe the same people who were going to eat upstairs in that dining room," said Tom.

"This is fantastic," said Izzy, bending over the chest and forgetting her fear. "We could take some of these clothes and show Dad and Great Aunt Winifred."

But at that moment, she felt that freezing finger of ice creep up her spine again. She stood back from the chest. Tom's teeth were chattering.

"I'm cold," he whispered.

Then suddenly, Izzy covered her mouth to stop the scream that rose in her throat.

She pointed to the far side of the cellar as a figure of a woman seemed to float right through the wal . The woman was wearing a long, black dress and her dark hair was pulled tightly back in a bun. She hadn't noticed them, but seemed to be searching for something.

"It's the g-ghost!" whispered Tom.

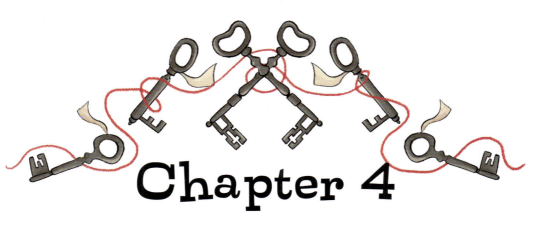

Chapter 4

All at once, the ghost woman looked straight at them. Her eyes glinted white in the torchlight. Izzy couldn't take her eyes off her. She was aware of Tom staring in the same way. Neither of them spoke.

Then, the woman reached out her bony hand. Very slowly, Izzy gripped Tom's arm and began to back away.

They had only taken a few steps when the loudest moan escaped from the woman's lips. As she moved towards them, she began to speak in a low, quavering voice.

"Give me back what you stole from me."

Izzy stopped. Her legs refused to move.

"W-what?" Tom whispered, staying close to her

"Give me back what you stole from me," the woman repeated over and over again.

Slowly, she came closer and closer. She seemed to be floating just above the ground. Izzy still couldn't move. She felt hypnotised by the ghost woman.

When the woman was just a few metres away, there was a shout.

"Fire!"

It had come from somewhere in the house above. It broke the spell.

"I can smell smoke," said Tom.

"We don't want to be trapped down here in this cellar," said Izzy. "Let's get away from here."

She turned from the woman. With Tom right behind her, she ran back across the dark cellar, past the old machinery and the barrels, and up the stone steps.

"Quick!" she panted. "This way."

On the lookout for the person who had shouted, they dashed through the kitchen into the hallway. There was no sign of a fire here. Seeing no one, they headed for the grand stairs.

That was when Izzy heard the rustling sound like the swishing of a curtain behind them. She realised what it was; the ghost woman's skirts. She was following them!

"Give me back what you stole from me," she groaned.

Up they climbed, panting and frightened as she climbed after them, coming ever closer. The cold of the cellar came with her, making them shiver.

The grand rooms upstairs seemed so long. Izzy thought they would never reach the door through to Great Aunt Winifred's house.

At last, she could see it, at the far end of the grand sitting room. With one big effort, they dashed through the room until they reached the door.

"Quick!" shouted Tom as Izzy stretched out her hand for the door handle.

"I hope it's not locked," she said.

Izzy pulled at the door then sighed with relief as it opened easily. They dashed through into the spare bedroom of Great Aunt Winifred's house. Tom closed the door behind them. Then they leaned against the door, gasping for breath and shaking all over.

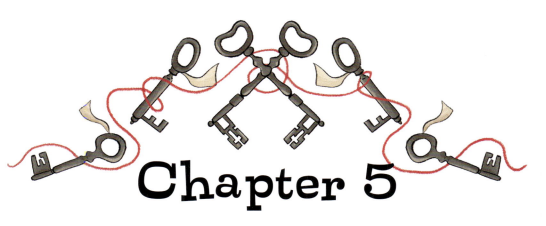

Chapter 5

"That was close!" Izzy said when she had regained her breath.

"I hope she can't come through the door," said Tom. "Like she came through the wall in the cellar."

Izzy swallowed. "I hadn't thought of that!"

But the only sign they had of the ghost woman now was the moaning they had heard before.

"I know she's terrifying," said Izzy, "but she sounds sad. I wonder what she has lost."

"Yeah," said Tom. "Whatever it is, she thinks we stole it."

"Let's go down and tell Dad and Great Aunt Winifred," said Izzy.

Their legs still shaking, they carefully climbed down the rickety stairs and burst into the front room. Dad and Great Aunt Winifred were sitting at the table, exactly as they had left them.

"Great Aunt Winifred," Izzy began. "We didn't know you had all those extra rooms in your house."

Dad frowned. "What do you mean?"

"Well, we've been through the door into the grand house..." said Izzy.

"Ah, that door," sighed Great Aunt Winifred. "I've seen it several times, but never found the key so I couldn't go through. I wondered what I would find if I could."

Izzy's eyes shone with excitement.

"Oh," she said. "It's amazing..."

"And we met the ghost..." added Tom.

"And she followed us..." said Izzy, shuddering.

"Stop!" said Dad. "This sounds like a load of nonsense."

"No," said Great Aunt Winifred with a broad smile. "Tell us more. I've heard the ghost many times, but I've never seen it."

"Heard it?" asked Dad.

"Yes," said Great Aunt Winifred. "It moans a lot and sometimes I can hear a few words."

"What does she say?" asked Izzy.

"She?" asked Dad, his eyes almost popping out of his head.

"Yes," said Tom, putting his arm around his dad's neck. "It's a woman in a long, black dress."

"A woman, eh?" Great Aunt Winifred gave Izzy a hug. "I always suspected it was. How exciting!"

"You're making this up!" laughed Dad.

"No," argued Great Aunt Winifred. "She says something about stealing... give it back... I can't remember her exact words."

"'Give me back what you stole from me?'" asked Tom.

"That's it!"

"I wonder what she thinks someone has stolen," said Tom.

"But how come we went through that door into a really grand old house?" asked Izzy. "We know your house is small. We can tell that from the outside."

"Aha!" cried Great Aunt Winifred. "You had better come with me."

She grasped Izzy's hand with surprising strength and pulled her out of the front door. Tom and Dad followed. They hurried along the path and out of the gate. Then Great Aunt Winifred stopped and turned round.

"See my house?" she asked. "Well, look at the left-hand side of the wall."

They all stared at the house. Izzy didn't know what she was supposed to be looking at.

"Look carefully," Great Aunt Winifred went on. "You will see that the bricks are a bit jagged, as if once upon a time, something was joined to it. And there is a piece of rough ground next to my house."

"Yes," said Dad. "I can see what you mean."

"Well," continued Great Aunt Winifred. "Many, many years ago, a grand old house stood on that rough ground. It was joined to my house, which was where the housekeeper and one or two servants lived."

Izzy and Tom gasped, looked at each other and nodded.

"Over a hundred years ago, it was destroyed by fire," said Great Aunt Winifred.

"Yes!" Izzy squealed. "We smelled smoke!"

Dad was still frowning. Izzy felt dizzy.

"That ghost woman might have been the housekeeper!" she said.

"Yes," said Great Aunt Winifred. "I agree."

They went back indoors.

"Did you remember to bring down that book from the spare room?" asked Great Aunt Winifred.

"Oh, no," said Tom. "We were so amazed to see that door through to the big house that we forgot."

"Well, would you fetch it now, please?" asked Great Aunt Winifred. "You might find it interesting."

Tom ran ahead of Izzy and reached the spare room first. As soon as he entered the room, he turned to face Izzy.

"Look!" he gasped.

The door into the grand house had disappeared!

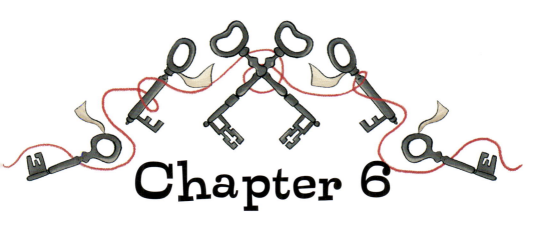

Chapter 6

The next thing that amazed Izzy was the book. It was large and thick, with a red cover. It was lying in the middle of the table.

"That wasn't there a few minutes ago," she said.

"I bet it's like the door," said Tom. "It just appears and disappears." He picked it up. "Wow! It's heavy!"

"Be careful," warned Izzy. "It's very old. It might be valuable."

"Great Aunt Winifred said we would be interested in it."

They hurried down the stairs.

"Ah, thank you," said Great Aunt Winifred. "I'm glad

you found it alright."

Izzy was eager to hear what it was about.

"It's a history of the old house and the story of the people who lived in it."

They huddled together with the book on the table in front of them. At the front, there was a painting of the house, which had been built in 1796. It was magnificent!

"Look at this part," said Tom, pointing to the side of the big house. "It must be where the servants lived... where we're sitting now!"

Great Aunt Winifred nodded, smiled and turned the pages so everyone could read the information. They discovered that several generations of the same family had lived there until 1888, when it was destroyed by fire. There were some paintings and early black and white photographs of the family.

Then, on one page, dated 1887, there was a black and white photograph of two women, which made Izzy and Tom gasp.

"That's her!" shouted Tom.

"Who?" asked Dad.

"The ghost woman," said Izzy.

Dad stared at her as if he wanted her to admit she was making it all up.

"Really, Dad," she insisted. "That is our ghost woman! The one standing up."

The photograph showed a grand lady in a beautiful lacy dress. She was seated at a little table. Standing beside her was another woman dressed in a plain, long dress. Her hair was pulled back off her face.

"Oh, how exciting!" exclaimed Great Aunt Winifred. "How wonderful, to see what she looks like after all these years."

Izzy bent closer to take a better look at the photo.

"But there's something different about her," said Izzy. "Look, Tom, can you see?"

Tom peered closely for a while then he sat up and grinned at her.

"Keys!" he said.

The woman standing in the photograph had a large bunch of keys hanging from her waist.

"Keys?" Dad studied the photograph. "What about the keys?"

"Our ghost woman didn't have any," said Tom. "She must have lost her keys."

Izzy thumped the table. "We've solved the mystery. That's what she thought we had stolen."

"Oh, I love this!" cried Great Aunt Winifred, beaming

at them. "I haven't had such an exciting day for years!"

"No wonder the ghost woman is upset," said Izzy. "If she was the housekeeper, she'd be in trouble for losing them, wouldn't she, Aunt?"

"Well, yes," Great Aunt Winifred answered. "The housekeeper had a very responsible job and she was trusted to look after the keys. I guess she could lose her job if she lost them."

"Poor woman," said Izzy. "So she has haunted this house ever since."

They turned to a chapter about the fire. Izzy read the information for a few minutes then she stood up.

"Come on, Tom. We'd better hunt for the keys so we can let the ghost woman have them back."

Before Dad could stop them, they had left the room and were racing up the stairs again.

Magically, the locked door had reappeared and the key was still in the lock. They stepped up to the door, put their ears against it and listened. No sound.

Izzy opened the door and sniffed.

"The smell of smoke has gone," she said, stepping into the grand sitting room again. "It must have been a false alarm."

"Good," said Tom. "I was a bit nervous of coming back into a burning house. Where shall we search?"

"Everywhere," said Izzy. "Let's begin in here and work through the house. Those keys must be somewhere!"

They looked under cushions, behind curtains and inside ornaments, but there was no sign of a bunch of keys. Their luck was no better in the dining room. They were just about to go out onto the landing when they heard a distant sound; the ghost woman's moan.

"She's coming up the stairs," whispered Izzy. "Hide!"

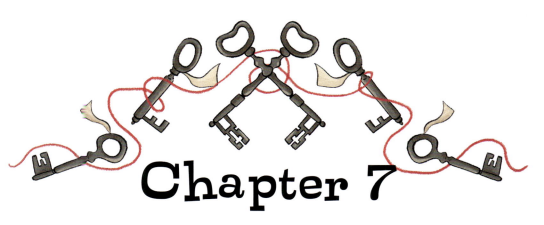

Chapter 7

They ducked down behind a large sideboard and waited. The swish of the ghost woman's dress grew louder as she came closer.

"Does she know we're here?" whispered Tom, closing his eyes and curling up as small as he could.

"I don't know," whispered Izzy. "We'll find out when she arrives in this room."

The door from the landing flew open and the ghost woman glided in. Izzy held her breath and kept as still as the furniture around her. The ghost woman came closer and closer then stopped a few metres from their hiding place. The icy draught made them shiver.

"Give me back what you stole from me," cried the ghost woman, but she wasn't looking at them and she began to glide away with a rustle of skirts.

Just then, Izzy heard the jangling of keys in the distance, but the ghost woman didn't stop. She went through into the grand sitting room.

"Now's our chance," whispered Izzy. She darted out from her hiding place with Tom following close behind. They tiptoed onto the landing.

"Shall we try those other rooms?" asked Tom.

"No, let's look downstairs."

"Not in the cellar?" Tom's eyes grew as big as saucers.

Izzy shook her head. "Let's go to the kitchen."

The jangling sound grew louder as they entered the kitchen.

"It's like a game I played at a party," said Tom. "The nearer you got to the prize, the louder the rest of the people shouted!"

Izzy nodded, but she was too busy looking for the keys to reply.

They hunted near the enormous, black stove where a fire burned and a kettle was steaming. They looked among the copper pans on the shelves around the room. But there was no sign of a bunch of keys.

Izzy sighed. They would never find them.

"Give me back what you stole from me."
The ghost woman was coming back.

Izzy ducked down under the big, wooden table and bumped her head on something hanging there.

The keys!

Quickly, she grabbed them and stood up. Tom stared.

"What shall we do with them?" he asked.

Izzy stood there, frozen to the spot as the swish of the ghost woman's dress grew louder.

"Leave them on the table," said Tom.

Izzy nodded and let go of the keys.

"Hide!"

Izzy ducked under the table and pulled Tom behind her. They were just in time. The ghost woman floated into the kitchen.

"Give me back what you stole from me," she cried then she gave the deepest, creepiest moan,

"Ohhhhhhh!
Ahhhhh!"

She reached out her long skeletal hands and snatched the keys from the table. Then, in an instant, she vanished.

Suddenly, there were shouts from quite close by. "Fire! Fire!" The smell of smoke returned. It was stronger this time.

"It's a real fire," cried Izzy as she leapt out from under the table. "Quick, Tom. Run!"

The smoke thickened as they rushed through the hall and up the stairs. Flames flickered behind them as they raced through the dining room and into the grand sitting room. Now the smoke was really thick. Would the door into Great Aunt Winifred's house be unlocked?

As soon as they reached the door, Izzy pulled hard. It opened immediately. They ran through and Tom closed it behind them.

They were gasping for breath as they hurried away from the door. A moment later, when they turned round, the door had disappeared!

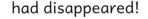

There was no sign of fire in Great Aunt Winifred's house. All was quiet as they ran downstairs. The moaning and jangling had stopped. The house no longer felt haunted.

"Well?" asked Great Aunt Winifred as they burst into the front room. "Did you find them?"

Izzy nodded. "Yes… and the ghost woman vanished as soon as she had them," she said.

"Thank you," said Great Aunt Winifred, giving them both a squeeze. "You're a fantastic pair. You've had quite an adventure. And you've made the ghost woman happy! She can rest in peace!"

Discussion Points

1. Where did the locked door appear?

2. What did Izzy and Tom find in the cellar?

a) A fancy party

b) A treasure chest

c) A chest of old-fashioned clothes

3. What was your favourite part of the story?

4. What was the ghost's connection to the house?

5. Why do you think the ghost chased Izzy and Tom?

6. Who was your favourite character and why?

7. There were moments in the story when Izzy and Tom had to be **brave**. Where do you think the story shows this most?

8. What do you think happens after the end of the story?

Book Bands for Guided Reading

The Institute of Education book banding system is a scale of colours that reflects the various levels of reading difficulty. The bands are assigned by taking into account the content, the language style, the layout and phonics. Word, phrase and sentence level work is also taken into consideration.

The Maverick Readers Scheme is a bright, attractive range of books covering the pink to grey bands. All of these books have been book banded for guided reading to the industry standard and edited by a leading educational consultant.

To view the whole Maverick Readers scheme, visit our website at
www.maverickearlyreaders.com

Or scan the QR code to view our scheme instantly!

Maverick Chapter Readers
(From Lime to Grey Band)